Walks on the Beach

Other Books by Sandy Gingras

What a Woman Needs

I Like You

Lessons of a Turtle

Reasons to Be Happy

Thank You

Walks

on the

Beach

Sandy Gingras

Andrews McMeel
Publishing®

Kansas City • Sydney • London

Walks on the Beach

Andrews McMeel Publishing, LLC

an Andrews McMeel Universal company

1130 Walnut Street, Kansas City, Missouri 64106

14 15 16 17 18 WKT 10 9 8 7 6

ISBN: 978-0-7407-9747-7

Library of Congress Control Number: 2010924511

www.andrewsmcmeel.com

www.how-to-live.com

what to bring on a beach walk...

bathing suit

cover-up

2010 beach

beach badge

big floppy hat

SPF 15

lotion

open heart

sense of adventure

muscles

cheap

lip balm

no worries

toe ring

Introduction

i 've been taking walks on the beach for most of my life. I've been looking for peace, looking for answers, looking for who I am. I'm a beach person. I look at the sea and I feel at home. But also, I look at the sea and I feel restless, provoked, inspired. The beach makes me want to walk. I walk to become someone better, to heal, to figure things out, to accept what I have to accept in life. I walk to escape myself. I walk to calm myself. I walk to feel myself in a beautiful place and appreciate the moment. And sometimes, I just walk.

I wrote this book because my walks on the beach have helped me in my life. I want to share what I've found. But also, I want to take you with me on my beach walks. I want you to have a little beach in your everyday, so that even if you can't actually walk on the beach each day, you can have a little beach in your heart (which is a healthy thing). So come with me, kick off your shoes, don't bring a thing . . . let's go for a walk on the beach.

Beach Walk Palette

warm
water

escape

Palm
tree

summer
sunlight

faded
beach
towel

sand
between
your
toes

weathered
things

tan
line

A Beach Walk Is For . . .

A beach walk is for stretching your legs
and your mind. It's to get outside yourself.

A beach walk is for watching birds swoop.
It's for seeing clouds change shape.
It's for looking at life with newfound eyes.

A beach walk is for bringing along a good friend
so you can talk about men.
A beach walk is for bringing a man so you can
    hold hands.
A beach walk is, most of all, just for you.

A beach walk is for healing.
It's for letting the sea and the salt air be a balm
for your wounds. It's for breathing in peace,
and letting go of disease.

A beach walk is for dreamy dreams.
It's for convincing yourself to go for it!
It's for feeling strong.

A beach walk is for jumping into the sea at
    the end
when you're hot and sweaty
and the water feels like a prayer answered.

Me and My Bathing Suit

It's just me and my bathing suit. I'm carrying nothing on my walk. I go off on my own and leave my family and friends behind. How often can we, as women, truly leave it all behind?

When I see women walking alone on the beach, I think, "Good for you—you got away!" Away is such an important place to be—even if only for a short while.

For years when my son was younger and I was a single mom running two businesses, I felt like I was splitting into many people, going in too many different directions. Time away was so precious then. I needed to escape to recharge my batteries, to remember who I was. These days, even though I'm less frantically pushed and pulled, I seem to still need a little "away time" every day. It gives me a little peace before the day turns into a whirlwind. It gives me a center of solitude and contentment and makes me feel more capable of dealing with whatever life throws at me.

So go to the beach with nothing—no wagon full of toys, no blankets, no beach chairs, not even a book to read. Go empty handed and come back empty handed. Feel how open you are. Feel how light you are. Give yourself a time where you don't have to carry the weight of anything!

Innocence

So much of our adult lives are filled with conditions. Even when we are taking a walk at the beach, we are wishing for more, or for something other—to own a house on the beach, or to live there year-round, or to have more time or energy or money to appreciate it. We can't seem to just accept what is—at its face value.

But take a walk with a child on the beach. It's the most wonderful thing! They accept what is unconditionally. They skip and hop in the waves and find treasure everywhere. The whole beach is a playground to them, the sea a magic wonderland. They don't wish for it to be otherwise. It is what it is—entire and sufficient.

Often times when I walk, I take my dog Quincy with me. He loves life with that same kind of childlike fullness. There's something contagious about a dog's pure kind of happiness. It's relentless joy, it's bounding, stretch-it-out, splash-around-in-it aliveness. Thank God for him. He lifts my heart up when my spirits are low.

So expand your
heart. Turn off your
mind. Open your arms
and accept the moment.
Take innocence with you when you
go to the beach, because innocent is
often the wisest way to walk through life.

Bulldozer

the nor'easter cut the dunes in half, left nothing but jagged cliffs and dune fence hanging down in shreds. I know what this feels like. I've been torn apart by my own storms. We all have.

Right now, the loss of a seven-year relationship has left me raw like this, my nerves exposed like so much rusty wire. Everything is in a tangle. I can see the layers of sand in the dunes, years of what's piled up and what's now torn down.

People say the dunes will come back ... to wait for the winds to shift ... that everything gets smoothed over with time. I know this is true. But there's a bulldozer a couple beaches down going back and forth, pushing the dunes back into place. I wish there were emotional bulldozers to save me some time, get me back in shape, cover up all the loss. Sometimes I try to be my own bulldozer. I sign up for trips and events; I fill my days with people and things to do. I know it's going to take time to heal, and bulldozing is just my way of trying to take control of things. But right now I like the sound of the bulldozer, its halting but stubborn push. I like to see it out here trying ...

Patience

Sometimes you walk the same path over and over. Sometimes you have to. Sometimes you can't see anything but the same thing even though life is changing all around you.

I keep going over the same memories, the same thoughts. I walk the same walk—down to the gray house with the red roof, turn into the wind, and walk back.

But the ocean won't let me make a rut. It smooths the sand out every day. Every day there's the hopefulness of knowing that I could make a new path. Every day is a blank slate.

I wish for these things: someone to come along and take me on another path, or a time when I get sick of myself and take myself elsewhere, or a time when I just start seeing it all differently. I don't know much about this process of healing. I know it involves a lot of change so small and incremental that you can't even see it as change. So I keep walking. I have to learn to be patient with myself. Not all change is about leaps and jumps. Some is very quiet. I think of vast tides turning one inch at a time, and how entire oceans move . . .

Green Jetty

that jetty extends far out into the crashing waves. It reminds me of how hard it is sometimes to reach out. How it's safer to stay within our own shoreline. But the things that are worthwhile in life are all risks: creativity, love, growth.

How exposed that jetty is. How naked. But how necessary. Without risking ourselves, we never discover who we are. We never see what we can do.

What is our life's purpose? We have to go and search for it. It won't find us if we are standing passively on the shore. We need to open our hearts and ourselves to the possible, throw ourselves into the chaos. We need to be jetties, risky and slippery and wild.

Wild Roses
and Beach Plums

the path that goes over the dunes is overgrown. There are bayberry bushes sprawling with their fragrant piney scent. Some wild pink roses are blooming, stirring the air with sweetness. The tender beach plums are beginning to ripen. I love these steps over the dunes, the crooked path, nature tumbling all around me. The scent of the sea wafts over it all.

The delicate things that grow on the rough edge of the sea are precious for how tough they are. This is part of being human. I recognize myself in the blossoms here, the reach and try, the delicacy in spite of the hard winds, the gentleness in spite of the harsh salt. That's the beauty part, isn't it, the bud opening in the face of difficulty?

When a Softness Comes

Life is hard. I go over the dune and the sand yields under my feet. It's soft. The waves curl around my bare feet. I'm walking. I know life is hard. It's also soft and gentle. *Don't forget*, every wave seems to say. *Don't forget. Both are here . . .*

Comfort: Bury my feet in the sand. Comfort: Feel the lemony sunlight brushing my cheek. Comfort: Watch the clouds puff along in the aqua sky. I walk slowly, breathe it all in. Comfort is embedded in the moment; it's everywhere.

Sometimes in the midst of hard, you have to look for the softness. Pile the moments around you like a blanket. Be conscious of amassing it. But sometimes a softness just arrives like a gift. A ladybug lands on the back of my hand. A dolphin leaps out of the wave. A perfect moon shell rolls at my feet. The beach is full of gifts, soft cushions in a hard world.

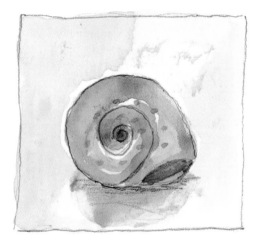

Horseshoe Crab
(Upside Down)

i find him wiggling all his legs at the sky trying to grab at something—trying to turn his life somehow. I flip him over, set him free at the edge of the water. I'm amazed how quickly he moves on. It feels good to have helped him.

We all have hands that want to help us right our course. They come out of nowhere. One moment we're stuck and vulnerable, then we're free. What seemed impossible suddenly seems doable. At a difficult time in my life, a teacher came to me and offered to read "whatever I wrote," a friend offered to be a partner in a venture, a stranger came up to me and said, "I read your book and it was important to me," a man told me he thought I was beautiful. They were all hands flipping me (the upside-down horseshoe crab) over and sending me on my way.

I have to learn this lesson: to accept the hands (visible and invisible) that reach for me, that give me new chances at life. And I have to learn never to underestimate my own hands and how they touch and change the world.

Collecting Myself

i walk to discover myself. I find myself here in that rugged little oyster shell (a hardened survivor) and here in that moon shell (mysterious and sensual) and again in the split clam (open and vulnerable).

I used to collect things on my walks, bring them home in my arms and my pockets. I have bowls of driftwood, jars of sea glass, shells in a bucket. I learned a lot about who I was by what I was drawn to: this + this + this = me. As women, especially, we define ourselves by what we gather.

Since then, I've gone through an uncluttering period (don't we all go through that when we realize we have *too much stuff?*). For, in an effort to define who we are, we sometimes bury ourselves in the process! But, take heart, the act of deciding what to keep and what to let go of is a process of self-discovery, too.

These days, I pick things up at the beach and then drop them. I want to find things beautiful and true, but I don't want to keep them. I feel that I have enough, and that's a freeing and

peaceful thing. Still, each day is a discovery. Each beach walk, I
find a metaphor to hold onto:

I am the broken moon shell
(and I'm feeling sorry for myself)

I am a necklace of whelk eggs
(and I'm full of possibility)

I am the clam shell holding
together by a thread of muscle
(and I'm clinging to the idea
of an old relationship)

I am a boat shell (and I'm an
adventure about to happen)

Each day, I'm finding the moody
clues to myself.

21

Storm

i can't walk on the beach today because there is no beach. The high tide is crashing against the sliced off dunes. It's hard to believe how the benign turns to chaos so quickly, how the gentle slope of dune is now a cliff.

It's like this: One day your mother is fine, the next day she calls to tell you she has a tumor in her lung. Cliff. One day your boyfriend wants to marry you, another day he says he changed his mind. Cliff. Hold your breath. Hold onto your heart. You're going over . . .

And if you try to climb up, it's slow and hard. You slide backward into pain, you lose your balance and your footing, lose your way. There's often very little to hold onto. There's the sky and there's the sea and there's the crumbling sand. Hold onto hope. Hold onto stubbornness. The only way back up a cliff is kind of sideways. So keep walking. Have faith that somewhere along the beach, there'll be a way up . . .

Be Strong

Walking is exercise. The more I walk, the stronger I feel. I like to feel my heart like an engine, a source of power. I like to feel the muscles in me working. The physical act of walking makes me aware of my ability to *move* in the world. It is so easy to feel stuck. It is so easy for our emotions and thoughts to stagnate. I feel like I need to move my body to convince myself every day that I can move the world a little . . . nudge it an inch more toward kindness. See, I don't want to just exist in life. I want to *live*. Isn't that what we're here for—to change the world? And that takes energy and strength.

Infatuated with Life

it's a summer day. The sand is crystalline and shimmery. The sea is aqua and warm and gentle and clear as sky. I'm walking around castles, around beach chairs pulled to the edge of the water. I'm walking in front of people reading and napping and smoothing Coppertone on each other's shoulders. Kids are darting in front of me. A toddler holds onto her father's hands and jumps the waves. Two boys are tossing a football.

The beach is smiling and romping. Everyone is on vacation. We all have ease baked into our skin, relax written on our hearts. There are moments when life is this simple. It's good to be infatuated with life. It's a beautiful day. Nobody wants it to end.

Sea Glass

Even the sharpest edges soften.
The brightest colors fade and cloud.
Things are fragile. They break.

Save the pieces. They're beautiful.

Invisible Currents

there are forces moving around us, calls we don't hear, invisible currents. The tides are pulled out, the wind stirs from nowhere, the butterflies overhead wing their way to Mexico.

So much of life at the beach is mystery. We are awed by the magic and magnitude of it all, the beauty and the power. With each walk, we plug ourselves into it, and we feel a part of something much bigger.

People always tell me, "You're so lucky to live at the beach; it's such a creative place." It is. Yes, the beauty is inspiring. And yes, there's the lure of open space like a blank slate. Yes, the vastness of it all makes me turn inward—to spirit, to emotion, to self-awareness . . . But there is also something about the beach that says, "Try to capture me—try to tap my mystery." We paint it and photograph it and write about it because we are a part of it spiritually, and we need to acknowledge our part in it, even if we don't understand it.

We walk, I think, because in many ways we're trying to make sense of our soul in the world.

Seagulls

the sky is full of birds, swooping pipers and diving terns and ducks going places together. Yet the seagulls are standing clumped up in a group on the beach, their faces bland, their backs hunched, some pout in their posture.

It's all about change. All the different moods of it. How exhilarating it can feel—the flash, whirl, pull of it. We've all felt that flying feeling. But look at the seagulls, how grouchy they are . . .

I feel like a seagull sometimes in the face of change. The fear of giving up the old, the resentment of "Why do I have to change?," the trepidation of the journey. Can I do it? I can get myself all hunched up like this, wings tucked in stubbornly, grumbling at anyone who'll listen, pacing around myself. I used to fight it, but now I know that this is the first part of the process of change. I seem to always have to go through this "seagull phase."

So, I give in to it. I stomp around and look at the sky, like "How dare you ask me to fly?" I do it till I'm sick of eating Doritos and someone else's crumbs. I do it till I'm sick of crying into the wind. Then I waddle away from my seagull self and get on with it . . .

Scallop Boat
(One Mile Out)

It's loaded down and riding low in the water. You can see the rust from here. It's a tough job, scraping the bottom of the sea to see what comes up. There's hard work being done out there.

But we all do a version of this in our daily lives—the chores and work and routine. We all live with the rough edges of life. And we live with the harsh edges of our emotional lives, too. Sometimes it's hard to keep dealing with it, keep going on.

But this boat on the horizon reminds me that there's something sacred in the work of life—in endurance and struggle and plugging away at it every day. It's an imperfect boat. We all are. But it shines in the sunlight. There's a rugged beauty to it as it balances on the horizon doing its hard work.

Split

S o many shells are really half shells—split open. Sometimes I feel split open, too—alone in life and incomplete, looking for my "other half" and feeling half-alive. Some of my married friends look at me with envy. "You're *alone*," they say, longingly, "you don't need anybody" . . . as if that's a good thing.

I guess it's hard to be a clam, and it's hard to be half a clam. But wherever we are in life, we're never half-people! Even when we've lost someone we love, even though we feel opened up and exposed and less than we were, even though we feel like we'll never heal . . . we're still somehow whole.

Look, this split clam shell lies open like a cup on the shoreline. It's holding life in its open palm. It has it all. And that one, face down and pounded into the sand, is lovely, too. It's beautiful even as it is struggling. They are both delicate and defiant. They are entire in and of themselves. They are perfect. If we could only see ourselves as whole, we'd be better at relationships (and better at loneliness, too).

Dribble Castle

i sit down at the edge of the water. The tide is way out and the water is warm as a bath. Kids are around me with plastic buckets strewn here and there, building walls and moats and digging pools.

I dig a little hole. I pile up the sand. Soon I'm making a dribble castle. I forgot how freeing it is to let the sand just drip between your fingers and pile up in uneven treelike shapes. Soon there's a little world of towers, crooked and silly.

I miss the child in me sometimes. As an adult, I forget to play. But it's freeing to make the castle, there's joy in building something out of nothing, the simplicity of it, the imperfect sweetness.

It's a Long Walk

i t's evening, and there's a wood fire going somewhere. I have my sweatshirt on and the air has the first hint of fall in it. I'm trudging along. I'm a stubborn thing. I keep on going. This has served me well over the years. So many people give up along the way. It's not that I have more courage than others or that I handle fear well. I don't. I just believe in trudging.

When I started my businesses, I had good ideas. But a lot of people have good ideas. An idea is just a doorway. You have to open that door and walk through it and then keep walking . . . on and on . . . and on. Most people give up at the doorway. They say, "It's too cold out there." They say, "I'll wait for someone to come with me." They say, "I'm not ready yet." I've said all of these things myself. Many times.

Then I push myself out the door. In some ways, every walk is a long walk. Just do it. Keep going . . .

Dawn

It's worth it to get up and watch the dawn. I forget sometimes how spectacular it is. How there's nothing but dark, then there's the glow of beginning, then the sun comes up like it's never come up before, glaring over the horizon like a ball of fire. It's almost spooky how strong it is, how it takes over the sky. It makes me believe in passionate new starts. It gets my heart going.

My life is filled with newness these days. I'm starting a new business. I met a new man. New is alien. It's like the dawn when the earth and sky don't even seem real, when everything is both strange and magical. I'm aware that I'm a very small being walking on a planet spinning through space. Life at dawn: It's scary. I'm at the edge of an undiscovered day . . .

What Washes Up

for years I thought I'd find a pirate's coin or a diamond ring. After fifty years of walking, I've found shells and driftwood, crab claws and skate eggs and, once, a dried-up seahorse. My dog finds round plastic containers that he can chase around and half-deflated helium balloons that he likes to pop and rocks he likes to dig up. We find treasure all the time, is what I mean.

Fishing Tournament

there are deep tire grooves in the sand where they've driven their beach buggies. Fishermen are driving up and down the beach looking for birds working. Looking for some intangible good spot. They get out and throw their lines. Reel in. Go someplace else, try again.

It's the annual striper tournament. Dreamers are everywhere. They've got buckets of bait. Good equipment. They're looking for dinner. But they're looking to connect to some current of aliveness, too. They're gazing out to sea. I'm looking with them. We all want to hook into life for one reeling moment.

Walking Backward

the wind is so strong that I have to walk backward. The sand is flying and stinging the backs of my legs. It's hard to walk at all. I'm going slowly, crookedly, feeling all wrong. I realize as I walk that I've been doing this a lot in my life lately—looking back at things, remembering, re-living, seeing only what's already happened, not what's happening now or what could be ahead. No wonder I'm not happy. I'm watching my life recede instead of approach. I'm living in my past.

Getting In

Plunge. Don't feel the temperature first, just headlong run, galumph over wavelets. Dive in. Done. Sometimes I get this exuberance and passion, and it's a rush. You take the risk of flopping, but, hey, you went for it!

But sometimes I stand on the shoreline and just look. I don't like the idea of just being a spectator to life. It's a fear of mine that I'll watch life go by removed and uninvolved. But there it is. It happens. I convince myself that "I have to get used to it first." But you can't *think* your way into life. It requires dare.

I watch the people at the shoreline in varying stages of getting in. In the end, it's all OK. We're all a part of it. Sure, it's good to be the one on the boogie board riding the curl of the water, in the rush and the froth of it all. But if all we are is knee-deep walking today, then knee-deep it is. Wade around in the gentle joy of it.

Low Tide

the beach has stretched out and out as far as it can go. Let me tell you, I think low tide is the most beautiful tide— inviting, gentle, open—female at its essence.

I see the women walking with their children on the shoreline, holding them, protecting them. So many women give and give until there's an ache within them, until they can't give anymore, until they are empty.

What we forget, as women, is that we have to fill ourselves again. And not with food or clothes or things, but with emotions that nourish our heart, intangible things that fulfill our sense of self. Even if we only give ourselves an hour of freedom, a walk on the beach, we are nurturing ourselves. We are giving ourselves a gift. We are letting the tide turn.

Stop Walking

In the middle of a walk, sometimes it's good to stop walking. Give yourself a pause. Stillness is a rare and quieting thing in the world.

I stop. I hear the *sshhh* of a wave, smell the salty air, feel it fill my lungs. Years ago, a psychic told me to repeat this phrase to myself: "I am eternally grateful for the abundance that is mine." She said it would bring me great wealth. And it has. Every time I say it I'm aware of all that I have, the sheer abundance of it, and the wealth of thankfulness.

So when you are walking, sometimes stop walking. Let the moment fill with thankfulness. It will bring you great wealth.

Fog

i can't see where I'm going, but I'm going for it anyway. I can only sense the ocean's presence near me; I can't see it. Everything is dense gray fog. My hair is dew-dropped and my face is wet.

All I can trust is right now, right in front of me. The whole world is the present tense.

I think I should give this new relationship a chance. I can't see where it's going, but I like right now. I miss the idea of having a future and a past with someone. And it's scary walking into the unknown. But honestly, we are all in a fog all the time. Although we pretend we can see ahead, we know nothing but now. And I know that life is about giving now a chance.

So I walk in the grayness. I feel my way along.

Sally, Dick, and Jane

remember that book *We Look and See*? For some of us, it opened the world up. Look and See. It sounds so simple, but it isn't.

Sometimes when I walk on the beach, I untangle myself, plan out my day, get organized. But sometimes, I don't want to think about anything. I want to just *be*. I focus on my senses. I smell the air, hear the birds, taste the salt, feel the breeze. If you can just *be* in the present, it is utter refreshment. It is a moment of pure aliveness. You get reminded that no matter what happens for the rest of the day, no matter what pushes and pulls at you and saps your strength, you can get to that moment again of being. The center of yourself. Look and See.

Full Moon

i love to walk on the beach when the moon is full and tide is way out. The sand glows and the water twinkles under the huge moon. I feel pulled and yearny and restless. Who could sleep at a time like this, who could be inside?

The moon makes a path on the water that I wish I could follow into the depths of green phosphorescence. Like a mermaid, I feel like swimming in the world.

Don't you love it when your spirit rises to the surface like this? Don't you love it when you can believe in your own magic? Walk in the moonlight. Dance in it. Run in it. Live as alive as you can.

Path

there are many paths to make on this beach, just as there are many paths to take in life. I am drawn to the people who follow their hearts, who make their own paths.

My son is twenty. He doesn't know what direction he wants to go in his life. Of course he doesn't. I tell him to take one step toward something he loves, then take another step . . . His road may veer and split and take off in many directions, but he'll know for sure that he'll end up in a place he loves.

In so many of our lives, we convince ourselves that *someday* we'll get on the path we love. We walk parallel to the life we really want to lead—the way of necessity or realism or fear. We walk on the paved road of other people's lives, when all we want to do is take a walk on the beach.

Go ahead. Take a step toward what you love. Life is the path you make. Walk your own way.